A Special Gift

For:

Angela Sue Woods

From:

Mom

Date:

Easter - April 23 - 2000

Dear Daughter

LOVING REFLECTIONS JUST for YOU

Brownlow

Little Treasures Miniature Books

Dear Daughter

Dear Teacher

Faithful Friends

For My Secret Pal

From Friend to Friend

Grandmother's Are for Loving

Mother—The Heart of the Home

My Sister, My Friend

Precious Are the Promises

Quilted Hearts

Quiet Moments of Inspiration

Rose Petals

Soft As the Voice of an Angel

The Night the Angels Sang

They Call It Golf

'Tis Christmas Once Again

You are a special treasure, a gift from God.

Dear Daughter

It has been said that a daughter is a
little girl who grows up to be a friend.
But you are immeasurably more than just a friend.
You are a special treasure, a gift from God.

Many of the pages you will understand now
and in the coming days. Some of these pages,
however, will not fully touch your heart
until you are a little older. Maybe we can
"age" together with love and friendship.

We make a living by what we get, but we make

a life by what we give.

WINSTON CHURCHILL

Gratitude

is born in

hearts that

take time

to count up

past mercies.

CHARLES EDWARD JEFFERSON

All the Good

Do all the good you can,

By all the means you can,

In all the ways you can,

In all the places you can,

At all the times you can,

To all the people you can,

As long as ever you can.

JOHN WESLEY

Making the World Beautiful

Every day I wish to make the world

a more beautiful place than I found it.

MADAME DE POMPADOUR

All the beautiful sentiments in the world

weigh less than a single lovely action.

ANONYMOUS

If the world is cold,

make it your business to build fires.

HORACE TRAUBEL

I used to ask God to help me. Then I asked if I might help Him. I ended up by asking Him to do His work through me.

JAMES HUDSON TAYLOR

God does not want us to do extraordinary things;
He wants us to do the ordinary things extraordinarily well.

CHARLES GORE

God isn't so concerned with delivering us out of the mess we're in as He is in seeing us grow out of the mess we are.

L. THOMAS HOLDCROFT

Never be afraid of giving up your best,
and God will give you His better.

HINTON

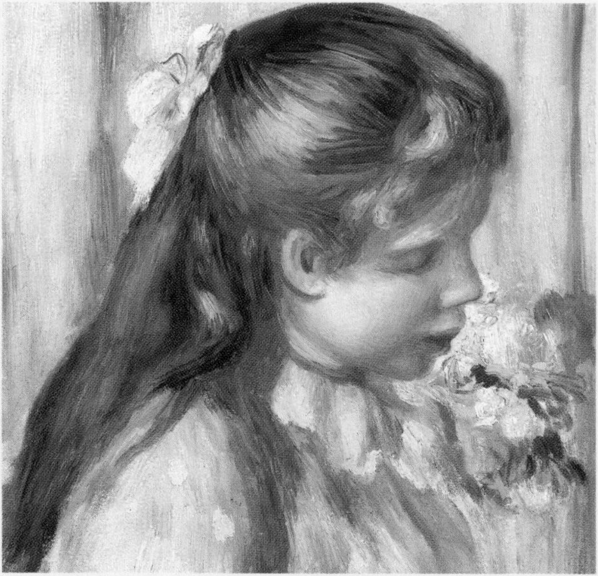

Don't worship the crowd,

your peers, your friends.

Expressing your individuality

by dressing just like everyone

else may not be so bad.

But there will be a time when

you will have to say "No."

Have the courage to be different.

We Are Not Alone

Wherever a man or a woman turns

he can find someone who needs him.

Even if it is a little thing,

do something for which there is no

pay but the privilege of just doing it.

Remember, you don't live in

the world all on your own.

ALBERT SCHWEITZER

The best cure for an empty day
or a longing heart is to find
people who need you.
The world is full of them,
if we will only look.

ANONYMOUS

We should never attempt
to bear more than one kind
of trouble at a time. Some people
try to bear three kinds—
all they have had, all they have now,
and all they expect to have.

EDWARD EVERETT HALE

Where Is Home?

Home to me is laughter…

Kisses on my cheek when they're least expected;

Glances filled with gladness;

The happiness in knowing

I'm a portion of

My family's fulfillment.

Home to me…is love!

JUNE BROWN HARRIS

Home to me... is love!

loving in love

When you love someone, you love the whole person,
just as he or she is, and not as you would like them to be.

LEO TOLSTOY

Whoever lives true life, will love true love.

ELIZABETH BARRETT BROWNING

Let love and faithfulness never leave you; bind them around
your neck, write them on the tablet of your heart.

PROVERBS 3:3

Loving allows us to live and through living we grow in loving.

EVELYN MANDEL

When you send out real love, real love will return to you.

FLORENCE SCOVEL SHINN

The Doors of Happiness

When one door of happiness closes, another one opens.

But often we look so long at the closed door

that we do not see the one that has been opened for us.

HELEN KELLER

The belief that youth is the happiest time of life

is founded upon a fallacy. The happiest person

is the person who thinks the most interesting thoughts,

and we grow happier as we grow older.

WILLIAM LYON PHELPS

Dear Daughter

Remember who you are. You are loved,
not only by your family, but by One
who loves you even more than we do.

How great is the love the Father
has lavished on us, that we should be called the
children of God! And that is what we are!

1 JOHN 3:1

Never get so fascinated by the extraordinary
that you forget the ordinary.

MAGDALEN NABB

Youth is not a time of life.

It is a state of mind.

ANONYMOUS

Be gentle and patient with people.

Everybody's bruised.

KATIE LAMBERT

Those who wish to sing always find a song.

SWEDISH PROVERB

It's never too late to have a happy childhood. —Anonymous

How to Get What You Want

If you want to be rich—give.

If you want to be poor—grasp.

If you want abundance—scatter.

If you want to be needy—hoard.

Becoming a Woman

One is not born a woman, one becomes one.

SIMONE DE BEAUVOIX

The family you come from isn't as important

as the family you're going to have.

RING LARDNER

No woman is truly literate who cannot read her own heart.

ANONYMOUS

It is only the women whose eyes have been

washed clear with tears who get the broader vision

that makes them sisters to all the world.

DOROTHY DIX

Prayer is not getting but becoming.

SIDNEY GREENBERG

Prayer is the contemplation of the facts of life from the highest point of view.

RALPH WALDO EMERSON

The Hands of Love

Love has hands to help others.

It has feet to hasten to the poor and needy.

It has eyes to see misery and want.

It has ears to hear the sighs and sorrows of others.

This is what love looks like.

AUGUSTINE

No clever arrangement of bad eggs
ever made a good omelet.
C. S. LEWIS

The tongue is located only inches away from the brain,
but it often sounds as if it were miles away.
ANONYMOUS

The most beautiful discovery true friends make
is that they can grow separately without growing apart.
ELISABETH FOLEY

If you don't get everything you want,
think of the things you don't get that you don't want.

ANONYMOUS

If you have made mistakes, even serious ones, there is
always another chance for you. What we call failure
is not the falling down, but the staying down.

MARY PICKFORD

You may trust the Lord too little,
but you can never trust Him too much.

ANONYMOUS

Dear Daughter

There are going to be a lot

of heartaches, insults, and pains.

Your enemies will do it on purpose.

Your friends will do it unknowingly.

Forget the hurts, the wounds.

Forget them all.

Being cared about is something so desperately needed
in this depersonalized world that people will crawl
across a thousand miles of desert to get it.

WILBER SUTHERLAND

There is a loftier ambition than merely to
stand high in the world. It is to stoop down and
lift those around us a little higher.

HENRY VAN DYKE

When we serve, we rule;

When we give, we have;

When we surrender ourselves,

we are victors.

JOHN HENRY NEWMAN

A Caring Heart

Be Good to Yourself

Many people go throughout life committing

partial suicide—destroying their talents,

energies, creative qualities.

Indeed, to learn how to be good to oneself

is often more difficult than to learn

how to be good to others.

JOSHUA LIEBMAN

Prayers of the Heart

Prayer requires more of the heart than of the tongue.

ADAM CLARKE

I have lived long enough to thank God
that all my prayers have not been answered.

JEAN INGELOW

Prayer must mean something to us
if it is to mean anything to God.

ANONYMOUS

Dear Daughter

You will have to make

a lot of important decisions,

even though most of them

may seem small at the time.

It will not be nearly so hard

to make them if you remember who

you are and what your values are.

Life's mysteries are for our worship;

its sorrows for our trust;

its perils for our courage;

its temptations for our faith.

JAMES MARTINEAU

The world is blessed most by those

who do things, and not by those

who merely talk about them.

JAMES OLIVER

There is in every true woman's heart a spark of heavenly fire

Every Woman's Heart

There is in every true woman's heart a spark

of heavenly fire, which lies dormant

in the broad daylight of prosperity,

but which kindles up and beams and blazes

in the dark hour of adversity.

WASHINGTON IRVING

Let Love Be Your Aim

What we love we shall grow to resemble.

BERNARD OF CLAIRVAUX

Any time that is not spent on love is wasted.

GOETHE

Where love is concerned, too much is not even enough.

PIERRE-AUGUSTIN DE BEAUMARCHAIS

Love is never satisfied with doing
or giving anything but the best.

J. M. GIBBON

Let love be your greatest aim. 1 CORINTHIANS 14:1

A True Beauty

Character contributes to beauty. It fortifies
a woman as her youth fades. A mode of conduct,
a standard of courage, discipline, fortitude and integrity
can do a great deal to make a woman beautiful.

JACQUELINE BISSET

Your beauty…should be that of your inner self,
the unfading beauty of a gentle and quiet spirit,
which is of great worth in God's sight.

1 PETER 3:3, 4

Dear Daughter

I really was your age once.

We have more in common than you may realize.

We both have the power to hurt or heal the other's heart.

We both need love and forgiveness.

We both want many of the same things out of life.

Let's help each other to get there.

It's a lonely road without a friend.

The person who sees a chance to do a good turn here,
and a little one there, and shed a little light here and
a little sunniness there, has something to live for.

HENRY DRUMMOND

What do we live for, if it is not to make life
less difficult to each other?

GEORGE ELIOT

Offer hospitality to one another…
Each one should use whatever gift he has received to serve others.

1 PETER 4:9, 10

Dedicate some of your life to others.
Your dedication will not be a sacrifice;
It will be an exhilarating experience.

THOMAS DOOLEY

For peace of mind, resign as general manager of the universe.

LARRY EISENBERG

Every person is gifted in some area.
We just have to find out what.

EVELYN BLOSE HOLMAN

"Thank you" are still the best two words I know
to express gratitude and appreciation.

ANONYMOUS

Every oak was once an acorn.

ELMER WHEELER

People who are wrapped up in themselves
make very small packages.

ANONYMOUS

What Money Can't Buy

It's good to have money and the things that money can buy.

But it's good, too, to check up once in a while and make sure

you haven't lost the things that money can't buy.

GEORGE HORACE LORIMER

Illustration Credits